Shadow
Dispatches

Shadow Dispatches

Polly Atkin

Winner of the
Mslexia Poetry Pamphlet
Competition, 2012

Seren is the book imprint of
Poetry Wales Press Ltd,
57 Nolton Street, Bridgend, Wales, CF31 3AE

www.serenbooks.com
facebook.com/SerenBooks
Twitter: @SerenBooks

ISBN: 978-1-78172-077-6

A CIP record for this title is available from the British Library.

The publisher acknowledges the financial assistance of the Welsh
Books Council.

Printed in Great Britain by 4edge Ltd, Hockley, Essex.

Contents

This Book

I am happy to announce this book is available.
This book is available in many countries.
All the source code that goes into making

this book is available. This book is partly
original material. Only in translation.
This book contains illustrations. This book

is available in hardback paperback pdf
hand-stitched spineless download in alternate
format large print braille Ancient

Greek and fifty-seven more languages
including two no person can speak,
as a cut-out-and-keep, as a sew-your-own.

Full book now available for free!
This book is an orphan. Adopt it. This book
wants ~~father and mother~~ editor. To be written

over. Here are some versions of this book
in natural languages. It is scratched in the rocks
with primitive tools. There are 104

extant theories of interpretation.
Its cover is a sketch of a bone-house, etched
as a robin's nest, eggs, chiaroscuro.

There is no tree to hold it, only
this book, which must be held down at night.
Its contents must not escape, whatever

form they take. This book is a killer,
is available, somewhere, always. Take it
please. This book no longer exists.

Colony Collapse Disorder

When I lived in the city I knew where I was,
what being there was. I knew I breathed
under a film of constant light,
that electricity was life. It moved
in my body, which I knew was an atom of the city,
and kept us twitching in unity. I felt
information bloom in my blood. It sang
in my cells as though it had always been there.
I knew without it I had no structure.

To leave the city was to leave one's memory.
Outside was a garden gone wild. Stars
were night-flowers in a mossy dome, opening
their dazzling mouths to amaze, spreading
exponentially the further from the city I went.
I knew nothing. What nothing meant. I feared
the dark and the space between things: space
needs filling. I'd cry for the city, its order.
To be let back in was to regain the future.

Now I live elsewhere the systems reversed.
The city is a picture from a book I once read
and nothing to do with me. Life is a movement
between dirt and sky. I see this clearly.
The stars are generators. Without them we'd fail.
Going back to the city is to speed myself up
to a drawn out buzz that I know is killing me.
Going anywhere other than elsewhere is rehearsing
this end: the shut-down of travelling energy.

All those years living inside weakened me.
Taken away from elsewhere I dim.
Friends visit and tell me that elsewhere is death
and the sky cannot feed me. Not indefinitely.
Their eyes are blown bulbs. They rattle. I smell
honey on their skin and know how it is.
When they move I hear humming like a swarm at a
distance.
When they speak I hear their voices, and under
the city quietly droning.

Worms

This morning between waking first and really waking
I found myself walking in a garden, barefoot,
through long cool grass still damp with dawn,
then saw, on sitting down indoors,
a dozen translucent silvery worms
had seeded themselves in my feet. I panicked
to catch them before they could root, pinching
their fish-hook tails between index and thumbnail,
flicking them out in one sharp snap,
like lashing a whip or unsticking a plaster.

With each worm drawn I discovered another,
their bore-holes like oversized pores on my soft pale
soles. Their pulsing bodies appalled.
I had not thought myself permeable. Yet
here were worms who had lived within me
for years, undisturbed, quietly eating me.
The older they were, the thinner they'd grown.
They could not sustain. They'd withered down
to loose strands of web, only visible
as I spooled them into the sun.

Kindling

It was the winter of fires that would not take,
of ash everywhere, never enough heat.
The winter of ice: opaque waves
creeping closer over the roads at night,
shutting you off from time and the outside.
Everything stopped. Your watch, your heater.
You piled all you could on your bed but still
the cold woke you at least twice an hour.
You dozed all morning. Afternoons you prepared
for evening, spent all your daylight kindling,
willing the flames to live; lost hours
crouched in the hearth, giving mouth to mouth
to the sputtering coal, praying for breath.
You knew you were just treating symptoms. The
                                    problem
lay farther than you could reach, no matter
how you contorted yourself. The chimney
was stuffed with the stubs of years condensed
into soft black snow that swallowed your stretching
arms when you went to clear it. It needed
more than you had; somebody trained
in removing the past. But this was the winter
you forgot how to use the phone, forgot
how to write a letter, construct a sentence.
You failed in the cold alone, speechless,
convinced it was something you'd done or not done.
By dark the room would be fully ablaze,
lit by laughing flames, denying
there'd ever been a struggle. Meanwhile
months passed, scrunched up like scrap on the grate,
and all that dead weight you ignored built up
like the frost as it kept getting colder.

Sky, falling

In the eaves of the ceiling above my bed
a hole is becoming. A web in negative
spinning itself. We're done with spiders;
there's only me here and scuttling matter.
Cracks fork out in the plaster like lightening,
a spiral of emptiness, pressing the air
into sheets and pushing. The outside is trying
to bore through my casing and let itself in.
It will win, no question. Its there in the pattern:
white split by black into segments, spokes
of a wheel which will roll down into me, whether
I choose it or not. It will move. It will move me.
It grows, a rose window. Blooming, it makes
this up-turned ship of a room, a cathedral.
It widens like an eye to the sky. It cries

build your telescope now and be ready. The stars
are weighty. The planets grow heavy. This attics
the skull of your wood and slate body. This hole
is your mind's observatory. Allowing it scope
is affording enlightenment. Space will drain in
as water drawn into a plughole, your soul
will swell like a seed in the rain, fat
with potential. Think how the spheres will peer in
as you sleep, and your dreams, so human and small
will meet their cold beams as they fall and enlarge
in their light fields to something immeasurable. It's almost
inevitable. All it requires is time
and the courage to give in to gravity, strength
to do nothing. Look! Even now the lid opens.
Lie back, and watch the sky falling.

Jay

i. feather

Gradating from white, bone-white of the quill-tip,
white as a dove's feather, deepening strand

by strand through every quiver of grey,
to charcoal to black to more than black:

oil on water. You could be plain
as pigeon, but for your brand, tattooed

on the darkest stretch, right of centre:
seven bright windows of pure ultra violet;

swatches of day in the night, blue-white
as snowlight, darkness between. By this

I know you. I know your name.

ii. body

It fell from nowhere.
I have never seen you

in the sky, in flight,
in a tree, alive,

only your feathers
fanned in a wheel,

small bones for spokes,
severed head fixed

like a pin in the middle.
You are not an oracle,

or a key to the sky.
But in my mind

when I think of your body,
you're not so much bird –

hollow relic –
as light.

iii. bird

Say I was waiting on the stony path
a long long time, seeing only my loss,

how I'd thought the body in air was everything,
how I'd thought of only how fine it was

to be the flare of blue in all weather,
and how death of course was to fall from the sky

never to regain height. Then
footsteps and you arriving. I watched

through eaten-out sockets, you photograph absence
as though it were something worth having.

I knew then we choose where we're chosen. You
                                        gathered
the small blue fish of my tailfeathers, slipped them

into your pocket like tickets.

The Glorious Fellowship of Migraineurs

When we gather we greet each other
by lifting tentatively one hand to one eye.
We meet in darkened rooms, quietly;
share no wine. Nobody speaks
but often our voices join to moan
the migraineurs psalm, low and holy.

The hours before fizz brilliantly, scented
with burnt toast and oranges, petrol, sparking
fireworks, fireflies, stars. Everyone
dons a halo, everyone's soul
shines out through their pores, whether unnaturally
small or wrapped in a skin of water.

We sleep the night together, slip off
one by one on waking from
a dream we pass between us, in which
the structure of the sky is revealed. We make
no dates, but palm to temple, salute
in a migraineur's kiss, our transcendence.

Somnography

Early this morning I got your note.
I can't recall the words or meaning,

only the light oblique on the screen
and how it made it feel, certain

transmission was real. I could recite
all the messages received in my sleep

which days have tried to prove imagined,
and one correspondence aborted mid-sentence

which sent itself nevertheless, as though
the content refused erasure, arriving

complete through the ether. We dare not believe
these shadow dispatches: corrupted, wishful,

impossible to delete. The same way sheets
I never strung to dry at a window

still fill the room with sails long after
I've moved, and how I'm still reading a letter

a man never sent, though I could repeat it
verbatim, clear as the sun through the linen,

billowing yellow and sweet as the wedge
that lit your words I can't remember,

or that email which backspaced even as I scrolled
down the face of the dream computer.

Potnia Theron

Our lady of animals, was it you in the meadow
in the mist where the calves grazed by starlight, their
                                                    breath
white globes in the dark? We stopped dead, sensing
shadow shifting, our own breath pooling
into phosphorous moons, feeling the deep
hush of invisible hooves, drifting
over the tips of the blades of the grass
as though skating on dew. When the first stag raised
its head and its antlers were moonlight, we knew.
Now every evening the freezing cloud skulks
from the peaks, we listen for the quiet of their feet,
to find you shivering on the drive in the shape
of a hind. Inside, we expect the glow
of your eyes at the black of the window, your furred
face emerging from the field of fog,
the glass between us. To want you is dangerous.
To forget you, worse. Mistress of wilderness.
In the old tongue, there were only chattels and *dēor*.

Mute

No grace in the nicotine yellow curve
of your throat, snakeish, its throb as you swallow,
open your toothed beak, croak, gutteral.

No grace in its muscular sway, in the way
you haul your body like a curse up the muddied
lawn, lumbering, clumsy. No beauty

in your antediluvian call. No music.
No love, no song at all. Ugly
as a god you crawl from the silted shore,

grotesque, hissing. We'd heard one night
you learnt the steps by moonlight, climbed
to the door of the hut and stopped, shocked

by your transformation, too almost human.
But there was no prince in you, no, no royalty.
Close up, only the leprous knob

on your forehead, your mark of longevity, bulbous,
crackled old leather, a slow black slug.
Can you eat pearls, isolate milk from water?

Now you have dragged yourself up from the lake
to show us your pain. Injured, you curl
on yourself and shudder. Mute as a myth.

We bring seed, drink, grow brave, creep closer.
Your fierce neck droops. So like a god.
Helpless, we leave you to suffer. Wake

in the grey light thinking of you, in the rain,
your threat display, your dinosaur motion.
And then I see it, your grace. The beauty

of continuation. You do not sing.
You build that low down growl you trill
like an aria, and we know you'll live.

In a dream a robin

In a dream a robin speaks to me from
the sill of the only window that opens
in the living room of the house I have just
moved into. He is too small for his name,
and seems more furred than feathered. He sits
still as I come to him, tame as a creature
in a Disney cartoon, us both unperturbed
by each others' strangeness. I turn in the centre
of the tiles and survey this place I've arrived at;
sun streaming in from four different angles,
rabbits hopscotching up the lane,
lambs springing over a ha-ha of flowers.

I kick in my sleep. Frost creeps up
the curtained panes of my winter cell
like a seal. Snow softly falls
over my bed as my breaths condense.
I shift and shiver beneath its weight.
When I wake the air has grown from grey
to yellow, warm on my face. I rise
and stumble through the house, drawn by a voice
more felt than heard, distinct as a piccolo,
piping me closer till I land in the centre
of the living room, blasted with light from all angles
and a slight sweet breeze from one open window.

Wrecking

The first week you lived in my life, you found it
full of things I'd lost or broken.
You couldn't understand why I didn't replace them.

You bought a brand new cafetieère,
although I kept saying I only broke them.
You didn't believe me, didn't reckon

on quite how careless my body could be.
That night in the car I couldn't stop crying.
Talk you said. I couldn't. I kissed

your mouth and my throat started closing.
I could see the road ahead but only
to the point of each bend, blue blue-grey

in the full-beam moon, though I knew what was coming.
We made a stop in the carpark of a pub
I'd only ever walked to. You wanted

to photo the lake lit up by night.
But the rain picked up and I couldn't stop crying
and the camera picked up close to nothing.

Later at home you adjusted the levels
and drew up the lake out of blankness, grainy
and beautiful. Mosaic. And you kept saying

she smashes cafetieères and breaks things, but

The bird that makes you afraid

You wear many masks. *Cat-eared hawk.*
Bring gifts, take the souls of children.

Your right eye placed in the hands of a woman,
sleeping, will make her tell everything, whether

she knows it or not. Your eggs eaten raw
cure madness, addiction. Your salted flesh

cures gout. If given to children – children
you have not stolen or eaten, children

whose mothers wore your image as protection –
they're safe for life. To ward off death

they may kill you and nail you to their door. Your hoot
is innocence lost, is a rhyme never spoken:

one for impending death; two
for success; three for marriage; four

for disturbance; five for travel; six
for arrival; seven for worry; eight

for death (sudden); nine, good fortune.
They covet your claws to climb to heaven,

circle your roost till you wring your own neck.
In the 1960s in the Pacific Northwest

they hung your effigy in support for loggers,
your threatened territory threatening theirs.

We will not harm you: you are our sister,
doctor, ancestor, messenger, sight.

To see as you do we eat your eyes.
Like you, when you ate your own mother.

Hive

For a moment I misread the instruction
and thought it wanted me to be a hive.
In my mind I saw a honey pot, some
glossed ceramic with static buzz
glazed in translucent amber, coiled
like a snake, a rounded pyramid structure
but built with a lid for a mouth, a wound
opening the skull on the soft brain matter.
It began to dissolve right then, mulched
in its own sweet juice – papier mâché –
a wasp's nest tossed on the compost, the storm
coming after. Neither a brewing bee
nor a building ant. I knew myself.
The whole pulp globe, collapsing corridor
on lacy corridor, my hairless legs
set firm in the hardening nectar.

Swimming

It happens one hour three minutes in:
the exact moment you slip exactly

into your body, just as your body
precisely pours itself through the water

without being ordered. You're swimmer and water
in equal measure, and also in neither.

You've swum for leagues, each stroke undoing
the other swimmers, Christmas, Scotland,

the tidy bounds of this hotel pool;
its lanes, white tiles, chemical soup;

away from yourself, pushing yourself
out of the body in time, sculling

three hundred miles through air and life
to arrive at a mountainside, two summers earlier,

hovering over a sparkling tarn
you soaked a blue day away in, alone.

To say how far you plummet you hardly
make a ripple, less than a pebble.

You dive-bomb ungainly graceful as a heron,
but land as yourself, particularly human.

You watch your dim limbs whitely glide
through cool brown depths, striped by sun,

while vast drowned forests of ochre ferns
sway below your toes, as though

you are very large or far above them.
A voice calls out. For half a second

you're both selves at once. Then the crunch
and one of your bodies is sinking.

Other People Dream of Foxes

1.

I wish you hadn't told me
the dream you had about the fox.

It hounds me like one of my own. Because
you told me briefly, leaving out details,

both of us vague and far from home,
the version that haunts me is set in the house

I grew up in, meaning the fox you had killed
was our own garden fox, the one we watched

lounging on the roof of the shed like a lion
surveying his dominion, gracious and unlikely,

striding straight out of our jumbled vision
to stretch himself out in the sun. It was

his unmistakable features I saw
peering over the back of the rococo chair

as though he had crept in to curl by the fire
as you sat, sleepy with winter, you

and my sister-in-law. In this scene it is Christmas,
the room full of candles and looking-glass baubles,

the fox-pelt staring with glassy eyes,
tail on the carpet like rusty tinsel.

Perhaps it's a catchlight that makes you start
and realise the danger, the creatures dancing

in its pupils, giving off sparks. Sister-
in-law says *you better get rid of it, quickly*

and so you do, the only way
you can think of, taking your lead from a story

you said you'd forgotten but must have remembered:
the friend of my brother's who set out to boil

a fox's head to the skull in their shared
student flat. He left it too long

and the bones dissolved to a thick grey soup.
With no time to lose, you dash to the kitchen,

cram the fox-fur into a pan
and set about stewing it down to nothing:

*those things in its eyes must be stopped! Imagine
the damage they'd do.* Imagine. It's not

this that I see when I picture it: you
steering a great wooden spoon round a cauldron,

but the look on the fox's face as he rests
his muzzle on the golden brocade, still smiling

as though he knows a secret, or is simply
amused to find himself finally invited

to dinner in his neighbours' den.

2.

Most girls make wolves into monsters. For you
it was always foxes: one more thing

we could never agree on, for all that sharing,
sprawled on our stomachs on the lawn, swinging

our legs like we were still children, or lying
in bed awake, whispering to the dark

things we might never admit by day.
That's when you told me your nightmare: fluid

foxes pouring through the keyholes of doors
you'd locked to keep them out, streaming

one after another after another, lips
curled the better to show their teeth,

a constant flow of incisors, dripping
with hunger, impossible to push back as water.

You were drowning in foxes. You woke up gasping,
and never shook off the fear of sinking

under the swell of fur. So vivid
it could have been me underneath it. Sometimes

I've thought it was: mornings I've woken
bristling, choking, stinking of fox.

3.

Stood on the station platform you squint
into the clear white light. Snow

low on the fells and the sky as blue
as your own side-lit eyes. Your chest hurts. Yesterday

frost so dense it held all day
against the sun, ice in the dips

of the path through the woods like annealed glass, thick
and clouded. Later you lay semi-supine

on the old road amazed at the stars. Cracked
tarmac cold through your coat, frosted

grass crackling at your hands. Somewhere
to the west of Orion's belt you saw them,

just as that morning, pink tongues lolling
out of their mouths as you let them pass.

Now here they are at the station, in place
of your train, shaking snow from their coats,

ghosting across the tracks.

4.

Through the computer you told me last night
I forced you to walk to the west of the lake

to collect the carcass of a fox from the beach
and drag it back in an old plastic bag.

It was heavy as a wet wool coat. It stank.
It left a trail of itself in your place.

You hated it, hated its weight. The sense
of light feet stalking your steps, on scent.

Hermes Enodios

Already you are scheming for the road, the road.
You have barely stopped moving, never quite stop
long enough for your words to catch up.

They are motes in a dust-cloud of ghosts in your wake,
or are flung ahead, fluttering overtures,
singing not theirs but your own lucky song,

so when you come we already love you,
have dreamt your dreams for moons in moons,
have rebuilt our homes around you.

You raise your arm as if to speak
or signal the direction you mean to take.
All rise to follow. You are the gate

between here and anywhere. All must pass through,
and only you know how to get where we're going.
You will take our best herds and best hearts when you go.

This morning, a fresh fall of feathers in the yard.
This evening, a swinging door, slamming.

Living in Attics

They know what it is, to live in attics.
To lie eyes wide that close to the sky,
unable to see it. To stretch themselves out.
Never to reach it. They feel the weight
of ceilings on them. Stars and planets

moving above like ghosts. They know
the orbit through fear and longing; they travel it
long dark hours, contained by slates,
depressed by the density of air and stone.

They dream themselves as water, tidal,
directed by winds, controlled by the moon.
Escaping everywhere. What they have learnt
is weathering: living, rattled awake
by storms coming in, thunder, planes.

Notes

'Colony Collapse Disorder' is the term created to describe the sudden unexplained devolution of honey bee colonies.

'Potnia Theron' is an epithet for Artemis which loosely translates as 'our lady of animals' or 'mistress of wilderness'.

The bird that makes you afraid is a direct translation of the Cameroon word for 'owl'. *Cat-eared hawk* is a translation of a Chinese word for 'owl'.

'Hermes Enodios' is an epithet for Hermes which loosely translates as *'Hermes of the road'*.

Acknowledgments

Acknowledgements are due to the following publications in which these poems were first printed. 'This Book' first appeared in *1110/3*; 'Jay' in *Flax 018: The Crowd Without*; 'The Glorious Fellowship of Migraineurs' in *Mslexia* 56; 'Mute' in *Magma* 53; 'Other People Dream of Foxes' illustrated by Craig Morrison's lino cuts in *Pilot Pocket Book* 9, and 'Hermes Enodios' in *Tellus* 2.

'Colony Collapse Disorder' won the 2008 Troubadour Coffee House Poetry Prize. 'The Glorious Fellowship of Migraineurs' was commended in 2010. '*The bird who makes you afraid*' was commended in the 2010 Basil Bunting Prize; 'Kindling' in the 2010 Wigton Prize, and 'In a dream a robin', in the 2011 Ashbourne Festival Poetry Prize. 'Sky, Falling' won the 2011 Kent Sussex Poetry Society Prize, and 'Swimming' was placed third in the 2011 Ashbourne Festival Prize. 'Hive' was short-listed for the 2011 Wasafiri New Writing Prize.